21 Ways to Become the Biggest Loser

through Fasting

CARMEISHA ARNOLD

© 2015 by Carmeisha Arnold
All rights reserved. First printing 2014.

This book is protected by the copyright laws of the United States of America. This book may not be copied or reprinted for commercial gain or profit. The use of short quotations or occasional page copying for personal or group reference is permitted. Permission granted upon request.

Published in Knoxville, Tennessee, by 8 STREAMS.
8 Streams
P.O. Box 34013
Knoxville, TN. 37930
8streamspub@gmail.com

21 Ways to Become the Biggest Loser through Fasting/ by Carmeisha Arnold

ISBN 10: 0-6923-7912-6
ISBN 13: 978-0-6923-7912-7

Unless otherwise noted, scripture references are taken from New King James Version. Copyright ©1982 by Thomas Nelson, Inc. Used by permission. All rights reserved.

Scripture quotations marked NIV are taken from the NEW INTERNATIONAL VERSION®, NIV. Copyright ©1973, 1978, 1984 by International Bible Society. Used by permission of Zondervan.

Scripture quotations marked MSG are taken from The Message, copyright © 1993,1994,1995,1996, 2000, 2001, 2002. Used by permission of NavPress Publishing Group.

Scripture quotations marked NASB are taken from the NEW AMERICAN STANDARD BIBLE ®, copyright © 1960, 1962, 1963, 1968, 1971, 1972, 1973, 1977, 1995 by the Lockman Foundation. Used by permission.

Scripture quotations marked KJV are taken from the Holy Bible, King James Version.

21 Ways to Become the Biggest Loser through Fasting   65p.
Includes bibliographical references.
1. Christian Life 2. Spiritual Growth 1. Title

Thank you H.S., friends, and family for always inspiring me and pushing me to move forward --- without you this would not possible.

This journal belongs to:

_____

Today, _____, I start my journey!

Introduction:

This journal is a 21 day fast companion, but can also be used alone. It is designed to help you receive the maximum benefits of consecration and move you closer toward the work and will of The Lord. In addition to inwardly committing to denying your flesh, outwardly decide to show your selflessness to others. Instead of focusing on yourself, invest in someone else. It's a way to live out what God's doing on the inside of you. Even if you choose not to complete a physical fast during this time, use this journal as a tool to gain greater insight into being the hands and feet of God. Most importantly, be sensitive to the leading of the Holy Spirit and allow yourself to be the vessel God chooses to use! These are simply suggestions to get you started on practically living out the scriptures. Be mindful that the Lord may want to use you in various different ways, be open to His call and the invitation to serve Him each day. There's a blessing waiting, not only for the recipient but the giver as well. For every day you offer Christ, you extend more of yourself. 'To them God has chosen to make known among the Gentiles the glorious riches of this mystery, which is Christ in you, the hope of glory.'

     (1 Colossians 1:27 NIV)

How to use this journal:

Each day comes with a *'Challenge for the day'* as well as *'promises'* of reward for your obedience to God. Before you start a challenge, go to the back of the book and select a promise for that day....write it down, changing pronouns to make it personal, and claim it as you complete each day's challenge. Assign that promise to your seed of faith and expect God to produce a harvest in your life through your health, wealth, wisdom, favor, personal insights and/or relationships. Use the 'thoughts, insights, revelations' section to write down what you gained, or notes on what God is speaking to you. Plan to do one challenge each day for three weeks. Some may want to take one challenge and do it several times a day or several times a week. Maybe you'll choose to complete each individual suggestion within a challenge before going on to the next. However you decide to use this journal, commit to completing all of the challenges, even if it takes more than 21 days. While your life's experiences may not have been made in 21 days, if you work at it, you can develop new life pattern and change your life forever! The best way to break an old, unproductive habit is to replace it with a new more productive one. I challenge you to use this as a behavioral/prayer journal of your journey to obedient life. Each day includes a promise of reward for your obedience.

God is faithful to His word, so accept the challenge to try Him at what he says.

Imagine how differently your world would look if a few of your friends, your small group, or your entire church decided to do the challenges together. On any given day, there could be hundreds joining with you in accountability, to promote the good of others. It just might start a revolution of people changing their world. Join me on this journey to see a little bit of heaven on earth.

"For whoever desires to save his life will lose it, but whoever loses his life for My sake will find it."
(Matthew 16:25)

The ultimate challenge is to become the biggest loser!!!!!

Inspirational scripture:

..."Is not this the fast that I have chosen? to loose the bands of wickedness, to undo the heavy burdens, and to let the oppressed go free, and that ye break every yoke? Is it not to deal thy bread to the hungry, and that thou bring the poor that are cast out to thy house? when thou seest the naked, that thou cover him; and that thou hide not thyself from thine own flesh? Then shall thy light break forth as the morning, and thine health shall spring forth speedily: and thy righteousness shall go before thee; the glory of the Lord shall be thy reward. Then shalt thou call, and the Lord shall answer; thou shalt cry, and he shall say, Here I am. If thou take away from the midst of thee the yoke, the putting forth of the finger, and speaking vanity; And if thou draw out thy soul to the hungry, and satisfy the afflicted soul; then shall thy light rise in obscurity, and thy darkness be as the noonday: And the Lord shall guide thee continually, and satisfy thy soul in drought, and make fat thy bones: and thou shalt be like a watered garden, and like a spring of water, whose waters fail not. And they that shall be of thee shall build the old waste places: thou shalt raise up the foundations of many generations; and thou shalt be called, The repairer of the breach, The restorer of paths to dwell in. If thou turn away thy foot from the sabbath, from doing thy pleasure on my holy day; and call the sabbath a delight, the holy of the Lord, honourable; and shalt honour him, not doing thine own ways, nor finding thine own pleasure, nor speaking thine own words: Then shalt thou delight thyself in the Lord; and I will cause thee to ride upon the high places of the earth, and feed thee with the heritage of Jacob thy father: for the mouth of the Lord hath spoken it."

                              (Isaiah 58:6-14).

Cease to do evil, learn to do well! Always practice doing random acts of kindness or as I like to call them...random acts of charity. 'And now abideth faith, hope, charity, these three; but the greatest of these is charity.'
> (1 Corinthians 13:13 KJV)

Day 1...... Feed the hungry

Challenge for the day.....Donate to or volunteer at your local food pantry, buy a meal for someone, or pay for another person's groceries or restaurant bill. Spend yourself on the behalf of the hungry, be intentional!

What promise are you believing God for today?

_____

Thoughts, insights, revelations.......

_____
_____
_____
_____
_____
_____
_____
_____
_____
_____
_____

Day 2.....Clothe the naked!

Challenge for the day…..Take this literally and figuratively! Donate gently used clothes to someone or an organization today and on a regular basis. As you are blessed, be a blessing! If you find your brother or sister exposed, cover them through prayer, don't continue to uncover. 'Above all, love each other deeply, because love covers over a multitude of sins.'
(1 Peter 4:8)

What promise are you believing God for today?

___

Thoughts, insights, revelations…..

Day 3..... Introspection

Challenge for the day.....Come out of denial about yourself. Mirror, Mirror on the wall... Put your face in the mirror and ask what it sees. The looking glass of God's word gives us a glimpse into our own shortcomings, heart hindrances, doubtful dispositions, and attitudes that don't 'look' like God. Look into His eyes and see the reflection that He wants for you...and actively pursue the changes needed to reflect Him today. **Don't blame anyone else for your delayed deliverance, spend this time looking at you! Ask God to show you the real you, not the you, you show others or want to be....but YOU, uncensored.

What promise are you believing God for today?

_____

Thoughts, insights, revelations.....

_____

_____

_____

_____

_____

_____

_____

_____

Day 4.....Family matters

Challenge for the day.....Don't deny or ignore your own relatives---these people are connected to you for a reason and are in your area of influence--so influence them! Don't neglect what you see around you and when possible, do something about it. Don't expect that they won't receive from you, expect that God wants to use you. If not you, then who? What does 'your' family--those within your bloodline need? Pray that God will give you compassion for your own relatives. Be faithful over a few and God will promote you!

What promise are you believing God for today?

_____

Thoughts, insights, revelations...

_____

_____

_____

_____

_____

_____

_____

_____

_____

_____

Day 5.....Resist the urge to fellowship

Challenge for the day.....Free yourself of outside distractions. Commit to your own retreat of silence by setting aside 1-3 hours of time to be alone with God. Spend time in solitude and allow God to converse with you. Without asking for anything, be silent before Him.

What promise are you believing God for today?

_____

Thoughts, insights, revelations.....

_____

_____

_____

_____

_____

_____

_____

_____

_____

_____

_____

_____

Day 6.....What's your Yoke?

Challenge for the day.....Identify stumbling blocks, personal hindrances, or weights that exist to hold you down—childhood molestation, rape, injustices, etc.—and exchange your yoke for His. "Come to Me, all who are weary and heavy-laden, and I will give you rest. "Take My yoke upon you and learn from Me, for I am gentle and lowly in heart, and you will find rest for your souls. "For My yoke is easy and My burden is light." (Matthew 11:28-30).

What promise are you believing God for today?

_____

Thoughts, insights, revelations.....

_____

_____

_____

_____

_____

_____

_____

_____

_____

Day 7.....Maintain the Sabbath!

Laborious, routine activities can keep us from a place of quiet. Sometimes we engage in activities or busy-work to keep us from sitting long enough to hear what God has to say. Quietude is not to be feared but welcomed as a time of recovery. It's permission given and an example set by God as He created...then rested. *Challenge for the day*.....Rest from all your chores but don't cease your work for God. Follow Jesus' lead when considering whether or not to engage in an activity on the Sabbath. 'Then Jesus said to them, "I will ask you one thing: Is it lawful on the Sabbath to do good or to do evil, to save life or to destroy?" '(Luke 6:9).

What promise are you believing God for today?

_____

Thoughts, insights, revelations.....

_____

_____

_____

_____

_____

_____

_____

_____

Don't hide behind the good that organizations or people you are connected to are doing... 'Let YOUR light shine before men in such a way that they may see YOUR good works, and glorify YOUR Father who is in heaven.' (Matt 5:16 NASB)
My prayer is that you experience His fullness and great joy as you use your hands and resources to serve His people. Be a light in this world, without any expectation of a reward from another person or beneficiary of your act. Just do it, just because, and God will bless you.

Day 8.....Emotional support

Challenge for the day.....Call, listen to, offer comfort, visit, or buy lunch for someone in a hospital waiting room, nursing home, or other confined areas like the prison system.

What promise are you believing God for today?

___

Thoughts, insights, revelations.....

___

Day 9....Satisfy needs of the oppressed

Satisfy=to fulfill the desires, expectations, needs, demands of a person; put an end to a want, desire or need by sufficient or ample provision; change the equation for someone else. *Challenge for the day...*

Satisfy the emotional, spiritual, and/or physical need of someone that's emotionally, spiritually, or physically oppressed. Be creative!

What promise are you believing God for today?

_____

Thoughts, insights, revelations.....

_____

_____

_____

_____

_____

_____

_____

_____

_____

_____

_____

Day 10.....Provide a safe place for the wanderer

Challenge for the day.....*Emotionally*—offer a listening ear, S*piritually*--evangelize= make an attempt to lead someone to the Lord. *Physically*--offer a hug to someone 'seeking' love and attention.

What promise are you believing God for today?
_____

Thoughts, insights, revelations.....
_____
_____
_____
_____
_____
_____
_____
_____
_____
_____
_____
_____
_____

Day 11....Afflict the soul

Challenge for the day.....Take something you want for yourself and give to someone that could really use it.

What promise are you believing God for today?

_____

Thoughts, insights, revelations.....

_____

_____

_____

_____

_____

_____

_____

_____

_____

_____

_____

_____

_____

_____

Day 12.....Loose the chains of oppression

Challenge for the day.....Release one who is financially indebted to you or release someone who has sinned against or offended you. As you do to others, expect debt cancelation on your behalf.

What promise are you believing God for today?

_____

Thoughts, insights, revelations.....

_____

_____

_____

_____

_____

_____

_____

_____

_____

_____

_____

_____

_____

Day 13.....Be mindful to forgive

Challenge for the day.....Write a letter letting someone go of the hurt they knowingly or unknowingly caused. Then read it aloud, deliver it to the recipient, or tear it up. If the person is deceased, still do this exercise of release for yourself because forgiveness is for you, anyway. Holding on, only hurts YOU!

What promise are you believing God for today?

_____

Thoughts, insights, revelations.....

_____

_____

_____

_____

_____

_____

_____

_____

_____

_____

_____

Day 14.....Maintain the Sabbath!

Laborious, routine activities can keep us from a place of quiet. Sometimes we engage in activities or busy work to keep us from sitting long enough to hear what God has to say. Quietude is not to be feared but welcomed as a time of recovery. It's permission given and an example set by God as He created...then rested. *Challenge for the day*.....Rest from all your chores but don't cease your work for God. Follow Jesus' lead when considering whether or not to engage in an activity on the Sabbath. 'Then Jesus said to them, "I will ask you one thing: Is it lawful on the Sabbath to do good or to do evil, to save life or to destroy?" '(Luke 6:9).

What promise are you believing God for today?

_____

Thoughts, insights, revelations.....

_____

_____

_____

_____

_____

_____

_____

_____

Oh! Teach us to live well! Teach us to live wisely and well! Come back, God ...Let your servants see what you're best at— the ways you rule and bless your children. And let the loveliness of our Lord, our God, rest on us, confirming the work that we do. Oh, yes. Affirm the work that we do!
(Psalm 90:12-17 MSG)

But if you would:
Day 15.....Untie the cord /yoke

*Challenge for the day.....*Release soul ties, hindering relationships, limiting/unproductive connections. As they are revealed, let go of the things and/or people that have oppressed, held you under subjection, or placed you in servitude. You may try an exercise of placing a list of those issues and the names of those individuals in a balloon, then literally cut the cord and release it into the air to symbolize letting it go.

What promise are you believing God for today?

_____

Thoughts, insights, revelations.....

_____
_____
_____
_____
_____
_____
_____
_____
_____
_____

Day 16.....Provide shelter

In Luke 10:25-37, Jesus shares a parable of one paying an inn keeper to watch after and care for a wounded traveler. *Challenge for the day*.....Cover someone's expenses for a peaceful night's sleep at a hotel, offer rest to the battered or distressed spouse. Invite an exchange student, foster child, or homeless person into your home. When you see someone hurting, don't look the other way and step on or over them. Look them in the eyes and offer hope.

What promise are you believing God for today?

___

Thoughts, insights, revelations.....

Day 17.....Stop pointing fingers

Challenge for the day.....Don't shift blame. Don't hide your mistakes behind others nor make excuses. Take responsibility for what is happening in your life. You can't make anyone do anything....the only person you can change is you. What are you responsible for, what changes can you make today?

What promise are you believing God for today?

___

Thoughts, insights, revelations.....

___
___
___
___
___
___
___
___
___
___
___
___

Day 18.....Refrain from gossiping

Challenge for the day.....Shut your mouth concerning others; only speak what you know to be true about yourself. Gossip is often subtle and seemingly innocent, but before you know it, it's happening. Today, choose to put your tongue under subjection!

What promise are you believing God for today?

Thoughts, insights, revelations.....

Day 19.....Avoid malicious talk....

Challenge for the day.....Watch what you say, choose to speak life! Speak only things that are edifying.

"Watch your thoughts, for they become words.

Watch your words, for they become actions.
Watch your actions, for they become habits.
Watch your habits, for they become character.

Watch your character, for it becomes your destiny."

Author unknown

What promise are you believing God for today?

___

Thoughts, insights, revelations.....

Day 20.....Refrain from speaking vanity

Vanity=excessive pride in one's appearance, qualities, abilities, or achievements, character or quality of being conceited. *Challenge for the day*.....Make a list of everything that God reveals to you about areas of pride and arrogance in your own life. Acknowledge it, repent of it, and commit to a lifestyle and mindset of humility.

What promise are you believing God for today?

_____

Thoughts, insights, revelations....

_____

_____

_____

_____

_____

_____

_____

_____

_____

_____

_____

_____

Day 21.....Maintain the Sabbath!

Laborious, routine activities can keep us from a place of quiet. Sometimes we engage in activities or busy-work to keep us from sitting long enough to hear what God has to say. Quietude is not to be feared but welcomed as a time of recovery. It's permission given and an example set by God as He created...then rested. *Challenge for the day*.....Rest from all your chores but don't cease your work for God. Follow Jesus' lead when considering whether or not to engage in an activity on the Sabbath. 'Then Jesus said to them, "I will ask you one thing: Is it lawful on the Sabbath to do good or to do evil, to save life or to destroy?" '(Luke 6:9).

What promise are you believing God for today?

_____

Thoughts, insights, revelations.....

_____

_____

_____

_____

_____

_____

_____

_____

"When you do something for someone else, don't call attention to yourself. You've seen them in action, I'm sure—'playactors' I call them—treating prayer meeting and street corner alike as a stage, acting compassionate as long as someone is watching, playing to the crowds. They get applause, true, but that's all they get. When you help someone out, don't think about how it looks. Just do it—quietly and unobtrusively. That is the way your God, who conceived you in love, working behind the scenes, helps you out.

(Matthew 6:2-4 MSG)

Promises...(taken from Isaiah 58:6-13)

- Bonds of wickedness will be loosed
- Heavy burdens be undone
- The oppressed will go free
- Every yoke shall be broken
- Thy light shall break forth as the morning
- Thine health shall spring forth speedily, He will strengthen your frame
- Thy righteousness shall go before thee
- The glory of the Lord shall be thy reward
- You'll call, He'll answer?...You'll cry, He'll say, 'Here am I'
- Light will rise in darkness, night will be like the noonday
- The Lord will guide you always
- He will satisfy your needs (in a sun scorched land)
- You will be like a well-watered garden,...a spring whose water never fails
- You will build old places
- You will raise up foundations of many generations
- You will be called the repairer of the breach
- You will be called the restorer of paths to dwell in
- You will be called the repairer of broken walls
- You will delight thyself in the Lord, ...and He will give you a place of honor
- God will give you a position of authority, ...and cause you to ride on the high hills of the earth
- He will feed you with the heritage of Jacob your father

The mouth of the Lord hath spoken it!
(Isaiah 58:14)

God is not a man, that he should lie; neither the son of man, that he should repent: hath he said, and shall he not do it? or hath he spoken, and shall he not make it good? Behold, I have received commandment to bless: and he hath blessed; and I cannot reverse it.
(Numbers 23:19, 20 KJV)

Paul writes, "If you've gotten anything at all out of following Christ, if his love has made any difference in your life, if being in a community of the Spirit means anything to you, if you have a heart, if you care — then do me a favor: Agree with each other, love each other, be deep-spirited friends. Don't push your way to the front; don't sweet-talk your way to the top. Put yourself aside, and help others get ahead. Don't be obsessed with getting your own advantage. Forget yourselves long enough to lend a helping hand. Think of ourselves the way Christ Jesus thought of himself. He had equal status with God but didn't think so much of himself that he had to cling to the advantages of that status no matter what. Not at all. when the time came, he set aside the privileges of deity and took on the status of a slave, became human! Having become human, he stayed human. It was an incredibly humbling process. He didn't claim special privyleges. Instead, he lived a selfless, obedient life and then died a selfless, obedient death—and the worst kind of death at that—a crucifixion. Because of that obedience, God lifted him high and honored him far beyond anyone or anything, ever, so that all created beings in heaven and on earth—even those long ago dead and buried—will bow in worship before this Jesus Christ, and call out in praise that he is the Master of all, to the glorious honor of God the Father. What I'm getting at, friends, is that you should simply keep on doing what you've done from the beginning. When I was living among you, you lived in responsive obedience. Now that I'm separated from you, keep it up. Better yet, redouble your efforts. Be energetic in your life of salvation, reverent and sensitive before God. That energy is God's energy, an energy deep within you, God himself willing and working at what will give him the most pleasure. Do everything readily and cheerfully—no bickering, no second-guessing allowed! Go out into the world uncorrupted, a breath of fresh air in this squalid and polluted society. Provide people with a glimpse of good living and of the living God. Carry the light-giving Message into the night so I'll have good cause to be proud of you on the day that Christ returns. You'll be living proof that I didn't go to all this work for nothing."

(Philippians 2:1-16 MSG)

Isaiah 58:6-14 (Message translation):

"This is the kind of fast day I'm after: to break the chains of injustice, get rid of exploitation in the workplace, free the oppressed, cancel debts. What I'm interested in seeing you do is: sharing your food with the hungry, inviting the homeless poor into your homes, putting clothes on the shivering ill-clad, being available to your own families. Do this and the lights will turn on, and your lives will turn around at once. Your righteousness will pave your way. The God of glory will secure your passage. Then when you pray, God will answer. You'll call out for help and I'll say, 'Here I am.' "If you get rid of unfair practices, quit blaming victims, quit gossiping about other people's sins, If you are generous with the hungry and start giving yourselves to the down-and-out, Your lives will begin to glow in the darkness, your shadowed lives will be bathed in sunlight. I will always show you where to go. I'll give you a full life in the emptiest of places— firm muscles, strong bones. You'll be like a well-watered garden, a gurgling spring that never runs dry. You'll use the old rubble of past lives to build anew, rebuild the foundations from out of your past. You'll be known as those who can fix anything, restore old ruins, rebuild and renovate, make the community livable again. "If you watch your step on the Sabbath and don't use my holy day for personal advantage, If you treat the Sabbath as a day of joy, God's holy day as a celebration, If you honor it by refusing 'business as usual,' making money, running here and there— Then you'll be free to enjoy God ! Oh, I'll make you ride high and soar above it all. I'll make you feast on the inheritance of your ancestor Jacob." Yes! God says so!"

Reflections

Notes

1. Dictionary.com (n.d.). Retreived 2013, from Website: http:www.dictionary.com

2. Author unknown. (n.d). Great-Quotes.com Retrieved Thu Jan 29 2015, from Great-Quotes.com Website: http:/www.great-quotes.com/quote/

www.ingramcontent.com/pod-product-compliance
Lightning Source LLC
Chambersburg PA
CBHW061248040426
42444CB00010B/2298